Sports Stars, Stats, and Stories

FORMULA [illegible] STARS, STATS, AND STORIES

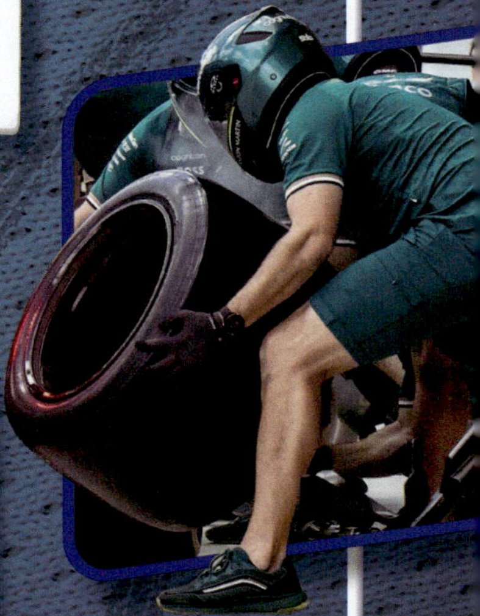

BY BERT WILBERFORCE

Enslow PUBLISHING

INVESTIGATE!

Please visit our website, www.enslow.com. For a free color catalog of all our high-quality books, call toll free 1-800-398-2504 or fax 1-877-980-4454.

Library of Congress Cataloging-in-Publication Data
Names: Wilberforce, Bert, author.
Title: Formula One stars, stats and stories / Bert Wilberforce.
Description: Buffalo, NY : Enslow Publishing, 2025. | Series: Sports stars, stats, and stories | Includes index.
Identifiers: LCCN 2024033668 (print) | LCCN 2024033669 (ebook) | ISBN 9781978542587 (library binding) | ISBN 9781978542570 (paperback) | ISBN 9781978542594 (ebook)
Subjects: LCSH: FIA Formula One World Championship–Juvenile literature. | Formula One automobiles–Juvenile literature.
Classification: LCC GV1029.13 .W55 2025 (print) | LCC GV1029.13 (ebook) | DDC 796.72–dc23/eng/20240815
LC record available at https://lccn.loc.gov/2024033668
LC ebook record available at https://lccn.loc.gov/2024033669

Published in 2025 by
Enslow Publishing
2544 Clinton Street
Buffalo, NY 14224

First Edition

Designer: Andrea Davison-Bartolotta; Tanya Dellaccio-Keeney
Editor: Therese Shea

Photo credits: Cover, pp. 1, 7, 13 (flag) hxdbzxy/Shutterstock.com; cover, p. 1 (car) motorsports Photographer/Shutterstock.com; cover, pp. 1 (Norris, pit crew), 5 (top), 23 (left), 25 (left) cristiano barni/Shutterstock.com; cover, p. 1 (tire marks) Litvinova Oxana/Shutterstock.com; cover, p. 1 (track) Kurka Geza Corey/Shutterstock.com; series art (banners) WinWin artlab/Shutterstock.com; series art (jersey texture) Kwangmoozaa/Shutterstock.com; series art (fact box background) Adam Vilimek/Shutterstock.com; series art (tablet) Lemberg Vector studio/Shutterstock.com; pp. 4, 28 Michael Potts F1/Shutterstock.com; p. 5 (bottom) Jens Mommens/Shutterstock.com; p. 6 AlessioDeMarco/Shutterstock.com; pp. 8, 9 (bottom), 15 (both) Jay Hirano/Shutterstock.com; p. 9 (top) FiledIMAGE/Shutterstock.com; p. 10 A.RICARDO/Shutterstock.com; p. 11 (Schumacher) Studio 1a Photography/Shutterstock.com; p. 11 (trophy) Morio/File:Drivers' World Championship trophy 2004 replica front1 2019 Michael Schumacher Private Collection.jpg/Wikimedia Commons; p. 12 cristiano barni/Shutterstock.com; p. 13 (top) kivnl/Shutterstock.com; p. 13 (bottom) Michael Potts F1/Shutterstock.com; p. 14 YES Market Media/Shutterstock.com; p. 16 Miroshnichenko Tetiana/Shutterstock.com; p. 17 (top) S.Candide/Shutterstock.com; p. 17 (bottom) National Archives of Norway/File:Fangio_in_1955_(cropped).jpg/Wikimedia Commons; p. 19 (top) ph-stop/Flickr.com; p. 19 (bottom) Nufa Qaiesz/Shutterstock.com; p. 20 Gregory Reed/Shutterstock.com; p. 21 (bottom) National Motor Museum/Alamy Stock Photo; p. 21 (top) Anefo photo colleciton/Netherlands National Archives, CC0; p. 23 (right) Independent Photo Agency/Alamy Stock Photo; p. 25 (right) Dijk, Hans van/Anefo photo colleciton/Netherlands National Archives, CC0; p. 27 (top) Lukas Raich/File:F1 Academy 2023 Spielberg Nr. 15 García (side 2).jpg/Wikimedia Commons; p. 27 (bottom) Jen Ross/Flickr.com; p. 29 imag3s 4 U/Shutterstock.com; p. 29 (bottom) Mark_studio/Shutterstock.com.

Printed in the United States of America

Some of the images in this book illustrate individuals who are models. The depictions do not imply actual situations or events.

CPSIA compliance information: Batch #CW25ENS: For further information contact Enslow Publishing, at 1-800-398-2504.

CONTENTS

Words in the glossary appear in **bold** type the first time they are used in the text.

FEARLESS F1

Formula One, or F1, is the highest level of car racing. Teams build powerful open-wheel, single-seat cars. F1 cars can go as fast as 230 miles (370 km) per hour! F1 drivers feel powerful **g-forces** as they round the turns of the trickiest tracks around the world.

F1's long races, called grand prix, are between 160 and 190 miles (257 and 306 km) long. For close to two hours, drivers try not to make a single mistake so their team can reach the **podium**. F1's history is full of exciting stories.

Get the Stats!

*In 2021, F1 began holding shorter races called sprints during grand prix weekends. They last about 30 minutes and are worth points toward the **championships.***

F1 takes a whole crew to get a car and driver across the finish line. Most F1 races require a stop at the pit, or a place along the track for fixes, tires, and other changes.

GRAND PRIX

As of the 2024 season, there have been more than 1,100 grand prix since the first in 1950. Grand prix have been raced on 77 circuits, or race courses, in 34 countries. Italy is the country that has hosted the most by far, with 107. Germany is second with 79.

Italy's Monza circuit alone has had more than 70 grand prix. The closest finish in F1 history occurred at Monza in 1971. After 55 laps, Peter Gethin beat Ronnie Peterson to the finish line by 0.01 second!

The curves of Monza, or Autodromo Nazionale Monza, can be dangerous at high speeds.

FIVE FAMOUS F1 CIRCUITS

NAME:
AUTODROMO NAZIONALE MONZA
LOCATION:
MONZA, ITALY

NAME:
CIRCUIT DE MONACO
LOCATION:
MONTE CARLO/LA CONDAMINE, MONACO

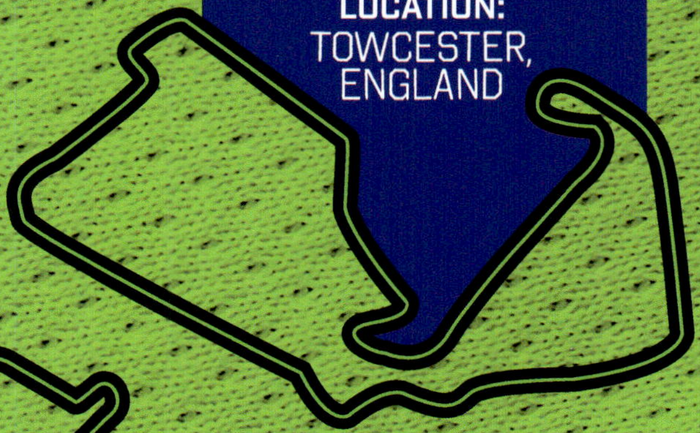

NAME:
SILVERSTONE CIRCUIT
LOCATION:
TOWCESTER, ENGLAND

NAME:
CIRCUIT GILLES VILLENEUVE
LOCATION:
MONTREAL, CANADA

NAME:
CIRCUIT DE SPA-FRANCORCHAMPS
LOCATION:
FRANCORCHAMPS, BELGIUM

HAMILTON ON TOP

If you want to argue with other F1 fans, ask them who the greatest driver is. This argument never ends. But some names are always in the mix—with good reason.

Lewis Hamilton of the United Kingdom has seven Drivers' Championships as of July 2024. He shares this record with Michael Schumacher of Germany. Hamilton also has won a record 104 grand prix driver victories and has a **career** total of 4,749.5 points, another record.

Get the Stats!

Sebastian Vettel sits behind Lewis Hamilton with 3,098 points. Vettel retired, or stopped racing, in 2022.

Lewis Hamilton raced with McLaren and then Mercedes (below). He signed with Ferrari for the 2025 season.

TALKING POINTS

The F1 points system has changed 30 times since 1950. Winners of some races in 1950 were awarded up to 8 points each race compared to today's highest amount, 25 points. So, points aren't always the best way to compare drivers.

Alain Prost of France was an F1 driver who raced mostly in the 1980s. He was called "the Professor" for his smart thinking on the circuit. If today's point system was applied to Prost's career, he would have seven Drivers' Championships instead of four. He'd be tied with Hamilton and Schumacher for the most championships.

ALAIN PROST

This is the Drivers' World Championship trophy, or prize. Drivers are given points based on how they finish in a race. How many points depends on the race.

Get the Stats!

Michael Schumacher has 1,566 career points even though he has seven Drivers' Championships. He raced when an older points system was in use.

MAX THE MAGNIFICENT

In 2015, Max Verstappen became the youngest F1 driver ever. He was 17 years old. At 18, he was the youngest race winner when he crossed the finish line first in Barcelona. Verstappen, who is from the Netherlands, won the Drivers' Championship in 2021, 2022, and 2023 with Red Bull Racing.

In 2022, he broke Lewis Hamilton's record for most points scored in a season, and he broke his own record in 2023. Also in 2023, Verstappen set a record for most consecutive, or in a row, wins with 10!

Get the Stats!

Verstappen started his F1 career before he had his driver's license!

Max Verstappen's fans wear orange, which is a color linked to the Netherlands.

MAX'S MIGHTY YEAR (2023 SEASON)

HIGHEST PERCENTAGE OF WINS IN A SEASON: 86%

MOST WINS IN A SEASON: 19

MOST POINTS IN A SEASON: 575

MOST CONSECUTIVE WINS: 10

MOST PODIUMS IN A SEASON: 21

MOST LAPS LED IN A SEASON: 1,003

ON THE POLE

In F1, "pole position" is the first place on the starting **grid** in a grand prix race. The driver in pole position—or the pole sitter—gets to start first. That gives them an advantage in a race where every second counts. To win pole position, drivers must have the fastest lap in the Q3, or the third part of a **qualifying** race that takes place before the grand prix.

Lewis Hamilton has the highest number of career pole positions with 104, followed by Michael Schumacher with 68.

STARTING LIGHTS

Get the Stats!

A hat trick in F1 is when a driver earns a pole position, a race win, and the fastest lap on a single grand prix weekend. Verstappen had a record six hat tricks in 2023.

POLE POSITION

In 2023, Max Verstappen had 12 pole positions—and won all 12 of the races.

EL MAESTRO

True F1 fans put Juan Manuel Fangio in the race for greatest driver. Fangio, an Argentinian, was a **mechanic** who first raced cars he worked on himself. His talent led him to five F1 Drivers' Championships in the 1950s.

Fangio was very well liked by drivers, teams, fans, and others. In 1958, he was kidnapped, or taken by force, by Cuban **revolutionaries** before the Cuban Grand Prix. His kidnappers respected him. They let him go, unharmed. Later, they sent him a birthday card that read, "From your friends, the kidnappers"!

MERCEDES
F1 RACE CAR, 1954

FANGIO'S 1951 ALFA ROMEO F1 CHAMPIONSHIP CAR

Juan Manuel Fangio won 24 grand prix with four teams: Alfa Romeo, Mercedes-Benz, Ferrari, and Maserati. Some called him El Maestro, which is Italian for "master" or "teacher."

Get the Stats!

Fangio didn't start racing in F1 grand prix until he was in his late 30s. He was the oldest driver to be a champion at 46 years old.

GREATEST COMEBACK?

Some say Fangio drove the greatest race in F1 history at the 1957 German Grand Prix on the Nürburgring circuit. He started out with a half tank of fuel, hoping he could pull ahead with a lighter car. However, at his pit stop, the crew misplaced a wheel nut. He fell about 45 seconds behind the Ferrari team. That put him in third with little chance of catching up.

Then, Fangio and his Maserati did the incredible. They broke the lap speed record 9 times over the next 10 laps to come in first!

Get the Stats!

At the Belgian Grand Prix in 1995, Michael Schumacher started at 16 on the grid. He came back to win!

Jenson Button's win at the 2011 Canadian Grand Prix, shown above, was a great comeback from 15th place. Two **collisions**, six pit stops, a **penalty**, and a thunderstorm couldn't stop him!

SIR JACKIE STEWART

Famed Scottish driver Jackie Stewart changed the sport of F1 perhaps more than any other person. A Drivers' Champion in 1969, 1971, and 1973, Stewart used his wins and popularity to work for more safety features in F1.

Stewart had seen many friends die in races. He believed a few simple changes could save lives. Among these were seat belts, helmets that covered the driver's face, safety walls on tracks, and **medical** crews at each race.

Get the Stats!

In 2021, the queen knighted Lewis Hamilton for his "services to motorsport." That makes him Sir Lewis Hamilton.

Jackie Stewart drove during a time when F1 was the deadliest sport. He worked to change that. He was knighted by British queen Elizabeth II in 2001.

JACKIE STEWART, 1971 BRITISH GRAND PRIX

TOP TEAMS

In F1, the driver alone can't win a race. It's a team sport. The race team is two drivers and from 300 to 1,200 other people, including car **designers**, **engineers**, mechanics, test drivers, pit stop crew, cooks, and many more. A person called the team principal oversees the entire team.

After the 2023 season, Ferrari is the team with the most wins in F1 history, with 16 Constructors' Championships. Williams follows with nine Constructors' wins. McLaren and Mercedes have eight each. Red Bull Racing has won six times, including in 2023.

Get the Stats!

The fastest pit stop ever was at the 2023 Qatar Grand Prix. The McLaren Racing pit stop crew changed tires for driver Lando Norris in just 1.8 seconds!

The Constructors' Championship (trophy shown here) is given to the team whose combined points from both its cars are highest in a season.

WHAT A WEIRD FINISH!

F1 has had some odd races. In the 1959 U.S. Grand Prix, Jack Brabham secured his Drivers' Championship by pushing his car across the line after it ran out of gas!

The 1982 Monaco Grand Prix was a series of unlucky events, including cars out of gas and breaking down. At one point, no car could finish. Finally, Riccardo Patrese restarted his car after it rolled down a hill. (Officials had given it a push away from a dangerous place on the track.) Riccardo was the only driver to complete the 76-lap race!

Get the Stats!

McLaren driver Lando Norris was at the top of the list for most podium finishes without a win—15—until he won the Miami Grand Prix in 2024.

LANDO NORRIS

RICCARDO PATRESE

Anything can happen during an F1 Grand Prix. Every choice on the circuit can change the lead.

WOMEN IN F1

Women can drive in F1, but few have—so far. The F1 Academy is the all-women racing class that began in 2023 to prepare women to enter high-level motorsports. Marta García won its first championship.

Hannah Schmitz, a head engineer for Red Bull Racing, makes important calls on the track, such as when to change tires. Her decisions helped Max Verstappen secure the championship in 2022 and 2023. Women have been named lead principals for teams too.

Get the Stats!

The first woman to compete in an F1 championship race was Maria Teresa de Filippis in 1958's Belgian Grand Prix. Maria Grazia "Lella" Lombardi was the first woman to score points in an F1 race in the 1975 Spanish Grand Prix.

After her F1 Academy win, Marta García joined the Iron Dames racing team in 2024.

FROM KARTS TO CARS

Many F1 drivers began racing in go-karts, or smaller cars with motors. Lewis Hamilton, Max Verstappen, Charles Leclerc, Lando Norris, Daniel Ricciardo, Fernando Alonso, and many others practiced with these smaller vehicles first. They learned about the importance of position and how to overtake another vehicle on a track.

F1 isn't just about speed. It takes brain power and training too. If this sport interests you, watch and study the pros at work on TV. Then, head to the track—the go-kart track—and find out if you have what it takes!

GO-KARTS RACED BY F1 DRIVER
FERNANDO ALONSO

Go-karts are a fun way to enter the world of motorsports.

GLOSSARY

career: The whole amount of time someone spends at a job.

championship: Events that decide the overall winner of a sport or contest.

collision: When two objects hit each other.

designer: One who plans how something will look or work before it's made or built.

driver's license: An official document from a government that allows someone to operate a vehicle.

engineer: Someone who plans and builds machines.

g-force: The force of gravity or acceleration acting on a body.

grid: In F1, the starting positions of the cars on the track before the start of a race.

mechanic: A person who builds and fixes machines.

medical: Having to do with care given by doctors, nurses, and others when people are sick or injured.

penalty: A punishment for breaking a rule of a sport.

podium: In F1, a raised area, near the start and finish line, where the top drivers are presented with trophies.

qualify: To take part in events that will decide which drivers will be in the main race and what position they will start in.

revolutionary: One who works to overthrow a government.

FOR MORE INFORMATION

BOOKS

Rains, Dalton. *Formula 1 Racing.* Mendota Heights, MN: Apex, 2023.

Stathes, Corbu. *The Best Drivers of Formula One.* Minneapolis, MN: SportsZone, 2024.

Van Cleave, Ryan G. *Lewis Hamilton: Racing to the Top.* North Mankato, MN: Capstone Press, 2024.

WEBSITES

BBC: FIA Formula 1 Standings
www.bbc.com/sport/formula1/standings
Who is the leader right now? Check out this site for the latest.

Hall of Fame—The World Champions
www.formula1.com/en/drivers/hall-of-fame.html
Get to know all the Drivers' Champions since F1 began.

What Is F1?
www.formula1.com/en/page.what-is-f1.html
Read these great explanations to learn more about this incredibly fast sport.

INDEX